CW00515424

VIENNA VACATION GUIDE 2023

The Ultimate Guide To Explore The Beautiful City Of Vienna

Bobby B. Turner

Copyright©2022 Bobby B. Turner

All Rights Reserved

Vienna Vacation Guide 2023

INTRODUCTION

Why Vienna Is Such A Great City To Visit

The city of Vienna, Austria is a must visit for anyone looking to experience European culture at its finest. From its incredible architecture, vibrant nightlife, and rich history, Vienna is sure to provide something for everyone.

For centuries, Vienna has been a hub of culture and art, and this is very evident when exploring the city.

Take a stroll down the Ringstrasse and you will be surrounded by stunning examples of grand architecture.

Vienna also houses very impressive museums.

When the sun sets, Vienna is transformed into a vibrant nightlife destination. For the clubbing scene, head to the city's trendy 7th district, here you can find the best clubs and bars in Vienna.

For a more casual evening out, explore the city's many cozy cafes and beer gardens.

Vienna also has an incredibly rich history, as it was once the seat of the powerful Habsburg dynasty. There are countless historical sites to explore in the city, from the Hofburg Imperial Palace to St. Stephen's Cathedral.

The city also has numerous churches and monuments, giving visitors a glimpse into Vienna's past.

Vienna's imperial practices, contemporary structuralism, vast history, and internationally recognized art and musical development have frequently propelled it to the top of lists of the best cities.

The ability of Vienna or Wien as the people call it, to accommodate is its most notable quality.

It disproves the claim that a person can only have one skin. Vienna frequently shows off its youthful and energetic side to visitors looking for the unsettling and the wild. Even beer is among the best in the city's nightclubs.

Vienna, on the other hand, is a tranquil city in general. Its demanding lifestyle, extensive history, palaces, cultural diversity, and rich musical and artistic heritage personify the city's flare.

Here are some reasons why Vienna is one of the classiest cities:

1. Vienna has the best living standards of any city in the world

Vienna offers a wide range of educational opportunities and a sophisticated public transportation network that locals can use for just €1 per day, and we feel really safe in this part of Europe.

The people of Vienna adore the city and are delighted by every visitor.

2. Excellent Culture

Vienna has a long history of creating outstanding classical music and theater. The city is linked to various legendary figures, including Beethoven, Klimt, and Mozart, to name a few.

For a place to talk about the day's events in a calm and picturesque setting, Vienna's coffee houses are beloved by both locals and visitors.

They have a reputation for being cultural hotspots where brilliant minds congregate because they were frequented by intellectuals, artists, and philosophers in the 19th century.

3. Classical Music

The Capital of Music in the World is Vienna.

Vienna's taste in music and enthusiastic participation in it makes up a significant portion of its cultural identity. Here resided more famous musicians than in any other city in the world.

I'm talking about Salieri, Schubert, Vivaldi, Beethoven, Mozart, and Mozart. The past of the city of music is filled with great names, but in the present, Vienna is all about upholding its musical heritage and producing fresher jewels for the globe.

Some of the city's notable musical institutions include the Mozarthauz, Schonberg Center, and Museum of Johann Strauss Dynasty.

4. Museums

If there is no place to preserve and record history, art, or music, what good is it? Austrians are aware of this and have made sure to carefully record, preserve, and make available to the public each significant component.

The largest art and music museums in the world are found in Vienna. Additionally, it boasts a number of fascinating museums, including the Sigmund Freud museum.

5. Residence

The most important thing is to always have a safe, sturdy roof over your head that is within your means.

Apartments in Vienna often check that option. Many boast of their polished parquet flooring, ornate ceilings, roomy interiors, and stunning exteriors.

Additionally, most people can actually pay the rent—a rarity if you're used to living in a major European metropolis. Depending on the size and condition of the unit, contracts can be set up to prevent renters from being charged excessive charges.

Prices have been rising steadily in recent years, but they are still low compared to many nearby cities.

With 60% of the city's residents living in apartments with subsidies, the social housing system has a good reputation. Homes provided by the council are occupied by 220,000 people.

6. Infrastructure and Transportation

Vienna has superb infrastructure and an excellent transportation system.

7. A Wide Range of Activities

You'll discover a ton of things to do, not just the well-known sights, whether you're a local or a guest.

There are several parks throughout the city, a fantastic spa, hiking paths, outdoor swimming pools, and other lesser-known attractions.

8. Pollution and Environment

The climate crisis is a serious issue that affects the entire planet, and towns all over the world are working to reduce pollution.

Cleanliness and environmental friendliness are well-known virtues of Vienna. It has been classified as having excellent air quality and very high ratings for both the quality and availability of drinking water.

Noise and light pollution, meanwhile, are both regarded as minimal.

9. Alcohol

What might this city's soul be? The preferred alcoholic beverage in the city is the Viennese Original Beer, not the Wien Wine.

At establishments all across the city, artisan beer and local beer are always flowing from the taps! The city of Wien is known for its vibrant nightlife, where you may discover its wild side.

10. Fantastic People

In actuality, Wien, as they name it, is home to some of the most fascinating people you will ever meet. Aspiring travelers, painters, and artists are all making their way to this alluring city.

Every person you encounter here will have a memorable tale to share.

11. Economy

Austria's strong social market economy has made it the 14th richest nation in the world. The World Bank noted that Austria has one of the highest GDPs (gross domestic products) per head, suggesting a good level of life for residents, through keeping close relations with other EU nations.

Austria's abundance of organic farms is anotherr aspect of the country's booming economy. It is commonly known as "Europe's Delishop".

CHAPTER 1

Location and History of Vienna

In Austria's northeast is the city of Vienna. The largest city in Austria, Vienna is also one of the country's nine states.

Vienna, the capital of Austria, offers a fusion of regal customs, music, and lovable charm. This is a city that offers both old and modern inspiration.

You can appreciate what a fascinating collage of architecture Vienna is if you take a seat on the adjacent Kahlenberg mountain and stare down at it.

There are lush, undulating vineyards and grand, imperial structures for which Vienna is renowned. After all, for half a millennium, Vienna served as the center for the writing of world history. Also, art history.

How To Get To Vienna For Travelers

Travelling By Air

Trains and airplanes are the two most popular modes of transportation to Vienna. The Austrian capital has excellent international connections because of its location in Central Europe.

Vienna is relatively accessible by air and land because of its central European location. The most popular means of transportation from Budapest or Bratislava to Vienna are via airline, train, bus, or boat.

Although purchasing flights in advance is frequently far more affordable, many people choose to travel between European cities by train because the inter-country services are typically regular and reliable.

From the United States

Only five American cities now provide direct flights to Vienna. Depending on the airline, many more have a number of flights with stops in many other locations in Europe.

Two stopovers may be necessary for flights from smaller U.S. cities, as well as from states in the west and south.

From Canada

On certain days, direct flights are provided from Montreal and Toronto to Vienna.

There are other additional ways to get from Canada to Vienna, some of which include making a stopover in a Canadian, American, or European city.

From Europe

There are numerous flights between Vienna and the United Kingdom, including ones that go directly from the main airports in the United Kingdom to Vienna.

Travelling By Train

Getting to Vienna by rail, bus, or boat can be a quick, simple, and reasonably priced choice if you're coming from a nearby European city.

The Wien Hauptbahnhof, Vienna's primary train station, has excellent local and international connections. It takes only a few hours to travel there from Bratislava, Budapest, and Prague.

The city has an outstanding public transportation system, so you should be able to get to your hotel and the sights from any arrival point. Trains from other cities might arrive in one of the city's stations.

Travelling By Bus

There are several bus stations in Vienna, including one for international travel right next to Hauptbahnhof.

Coach trips from adjacent cities are typically a bit more expensive but take longer than alternative train trips.

Travelling By Boat

Between Bratislava and Vienna, a boat service is conducted by Twin City Liners. 75 minutes are spent traveling, and each way costs between 20 and 35 euros.

The boats often operate in the summer and provide extra seasonal travel options for anyone organizing trips between the cities in the winter.

CHAPTER 2

Packing For Vienna

What to bring for a trip to Vienna? As with any other location, it all depends on your travel dates, your plans for Vienna, and whether you'll be taking any excursions beyond the city.

To put it simply, what you bring for your vacation to Vienna will mostly depend on the season and the occasion.

The weather will have a big impact on your trip to Vienna, so be sure to pack accordingly. Bring a travel umbrella, as it can rain in the middle of the summer, it will undoubtedly rain in spring and autumn (fall), and if it is not snowing in winter, you might get some icy rain.

What to Pack No Matter the Season or the Occasion

Here is a list of things that are handy regardless of the season or reason for a trip to Vienna:

- There are numerous types of travel power adapters; in this case, the one that can convert to a European power outlet (two-pin, Type C, E, or F)

- Power banks are helpful for on-the-go charging of your phone, tablet, or camera. Novelty solar chargers are also available; they can be very useful.

- Travel umbrella: A foldable, portable umbrella that doesn't take up a lot of room.

- A camera and a camera bag, just in case you decide to use something other than your smartphone to snap pictures.

- A little first aid bag that contains only what is absolutely necessary, like bandages, band-aids, insect repellant, and painkillers.

- Undies and socks (including travel socks for long flights)

- Additions (makeup, fashion accessories, etc)

Summer And Spring

Apart from Christmas, spring and summer are the most popular times to visit Vienna. These seasons can have good weather, however, there are often showers and temperature changes during the day.

This means that even in the middle of summer, you should pack a light jacket and some long sleeve clothing for going outside, especially at night. The following is a list of what to bring when you go in the spring or summer:

- Comfy footwear. The majority of Vienna's top attractions are close by and the city is fairly walkable. It is essential to wear comfy shoes. For spring and summer, you can wear sandals, dress shoes, or sports shoes.

- Short- and long-sleeved T-shirts. When the weather abruptly changes at night, this would be quite helpful.

- Shirts for evening activities

- Nighttime light sweater

- A pair of posh shoes for an evening out

- Leggings, summer dresses, pants, skirts, or evening clothing that is more formal.

- Hats to shield your head from the sun

- A lightweight jacket for the evenings or in case of a downpour when it gets chilly

- Sunblock

- Eyewear

Autumn And Winter

With the exception of the Christmas (markets), ball season, and on the route to a ski resort, autumn and winter are not particularly popular times to visit Vienna.

The end of October sees a significant change in the weather, and November is already rather cold with a lot of rain and chilly winds. The objective is to pack for the season so that you may still enjoy Vienna and its attractions, notably the museums and galleries.

The following is a list of items to bring if you're visiting Vienna in the colder months:

- Comfy shoes. There are also some perhaps waterproof shoes that are better suited for rain and cold weather.

- Pullovers

- Waterproof socks

- A pair of posh shoes for an evening out

- Clothes that are more formal for evening wear, such as pants, skirts, dresses, etc.

- Winter walking accessories such as hats, gloves, and scarves

- Waterproof and windproof winter jacket

- Thermal underwear, particularly if traveling outside Vienna

To protect yourself from the cold and wind during the winter, layering your clothing is strongly advised.

How To Dress For Sightseeing

Wear relaxed clothing and footwear when sightseeing in any climate. If you plan to spend the entire day sightseeing, you might want to pack extra clothing in case. When preparing for a trip to Vienna, keep this in mind. Consider this when packing as well because some attractions, including churches and cathedrals, may have clothing requirements.

How to Dress For An Outing

We may presume that you will engage in some outdoor activities given the abundance of walking-friendly parks in Vienna and the proximity of national parks.

This will call for extra athletic clothing, hiking boots, backpacks, and other necessary items. When walking in outdoors while wearing shorts or a skirt, be aware of ticks in the grass and use insect repellent.

Attending A Nighttime Event

After completing all the touristic activities, you'll likely want to unwind in the evening by going out for a drink, a nice dinner, or hitting the clubs.

Every one of these establishments, especially clubs, will have a specific dress code, so if you want to experience Vienna's nightlife, you'll need to pack some sexier attire.

Going to the Vienna Opera

The Vienna Opera has a lax dress code, so you don't need to wear a tuxedo or a gala gown to an opera performance, but your attire shouldn't be too casual either.

Both an opera and a theater visit would be appropriate in evening wear and a suit with a tie.

How to Dress for Gala Dinners, Weddings, and Other Upscale Events

If you intend to attend one of these events in Vienna, there is a specified dress code, and casual attire will not do.

You have two choices while in Vienna: to buy or to rent gala dresses, tuxedos, and other high-fashion attire unless you are bringing them with you.

Finding appropriate fancy clothing shouldn't be a problem for any style or body type because Vienna is renowned for having its own fashion business.

Depending on when you're visiting and what you have planned, you'll need to decide what to bring for Vienna.

What To Know Before Traveling To Vienna

1. Travel is not cost-free

Because there is no ticket collector, person, or machine in Vienna, many visitors mistakenly believe that transportation is completely free.

But in order to avoid a €103 fine, you MUST buy a transportation ticket. A single ticket is €2.30. If you receive the expensive fine rather than the inexpensive ticket, you will be kicking yourself.

Additionally, 24-, 48-, 72-, and weekly passes are available. Just BUY a ticket, please! They can be found near any UBahn stop.

2. Resign from your seat

When an elderly person, a mother with young children, or a person who is blind or physically disabled board any type of public transportation, it is customary to give up your seat.

3. The water is generally of high quality

Austrians take great pride in the high caliber of their water. Ask for tap water in restaurants or use any water fountain or sink. The Austrian Alps are the source of the water!

4. When shopping for food or clothing, bring your own bag

Most businesses charge customers for bags, so do your part for the environment and bring a recyclable bag.

5. Practice asking people if they speak English by saying "sprechen sie englisch" before you start a conversation

Even though many people, especially in the First District, speak English, at least introduce yourself with this wording rather than assuming that everyone does.

6. Sundays are largely off-limits to shopping

Sunday might be a good day to arrive if you're visiting Vienna because nearly everything is closed on that day.

7. Smoking

Getting used to the prevalence of smoking in Vienna is one of the biggest adjustments when visiting the city.

This act is not permitted inside, but if you are seated outside in a café or restaurant, there is a good probability that someone is smoking.

8. Taking alcohol in public

Speaking of vices, Viennese are typically permitted to consume alcohol in public. Of course, you have to be of legal age.

Therefore, it is completely usual to see individuals outside of venues or along the river with open beer cans.

Of course, there are many exceptions, like when using public transportation.

Basically, keep using your common sense, but be aware that you can drink a beer in a place like Lichterfest without running afoul of the law.

9. Gratuity

What the local customs are regarding tipping is one of the typical queries that come up when visiting a new place.

Travelers frequently encounter this issue because tipping customs tend to vary greatly throughout European nations and even between individual cities.

Tell the waiter how much you intend to pay, including the tip.

10.   The Vienna language

English speakers frequently assume that Austrians speak German identically to Germans, however, this assumption is only partially accurate.

If you don't speak German, the regional dialect, known as wienerisch, might not sound all that different. However, things could sound a little funny if you took High German in school.

Locals have their own terminology in addition to using various pronunciation emphases and sounds.

11. Christmas and winter

The period leading up to Christmas is one of Vienna's busiest times of the year, which may come as a surprise. Christmas markets start to develop in every square starting in mid-November.

Even if there won't be much snow at this point in the season, it's still a special time to visit Vienna.

12.   Festivals in Vienna

Of course, Vienna enthusiastically celebrates other holidays as well. Vienna especially enjoys its festivals, and whenever an event is taking place, there is always a lot of curiosity and engagement.

13. Free museum days

There is no denying that Vienna is a very cultural city and that it is filled with museums and art galleries. In fact, Vienna has a dedicated museum quarter.

In essence, there are so many things to do in Vienna that you could easily spend days just touring museums.

14. Opening Hours

Except for the shops at train stations and museums, almost all stores are closed on Sundays and major holidays.

15. Currency and Money

Austria as a whole and Vienna use the Euro as its currency. Credit and debit cards are accepted at the majority of places, including stores, pubs, restaurants, museums, and hotels.

It is preferable to use your Visa or Mastercard in Europe as American Express is not generally accepted there.

If you'd rather use cash, ATM bank machines offer the greatest conversion rates and often charge about $3 to $5 each transaction.

Vienna Weather

Vienna experiences sunny summers, and snowy winters.

The average annual temperature ranges from 27°F to 79°F, with rarely readings below 13°F or above 89°F.

Best Time To Travel To Vienna

Vienna is best visited in April through May or in September through October. In the spring and fall, there aren't many people around.

The majority of travelers come to Vienna in the summer to take advantage of the pleasant, bright weather. You can anticipate the city to become overcrowded and for accommodation rates to soar between June and August.

Although the freezing weather can be a hindrance, December also experiences a rise in tourism as many Europeans rush to the city for a taste of Christmas cheer served Viennese-style.

Bobby B. Turner

CHAPTER 3

Using the Bus to Get Around in Vienna

Vienna has a sophisticated public transportation system. You can get practically any where in the city in no time at all with the help of buses, trains, trams, and subterranean lines.

The public transportation system in Vienna, Wiener Linien, runs 127 bus lines, 24 of which are night lines, 29 tram lines, and five underground lines.

Only between 0.3 and 5 in the morning do night lines run. The Vienna subway is open all night on weekends and holidays for the convenience of its users.

Currently, there are more than 450 buses and over 500 tramcars in the Wiener Linien vehicle fleet. The price of one ticket is EUR 2.40.

Where can I buy tickets?

• most subway stations have ticket machines

• points of sale in advance

• Tickets are also sold by tobacconists

• at an enhanced rate of EUR 2.60 for each ticket when riding the tram

Passes

There are passes available in addition to single tickets, hourly passes as well as weekly, monthly, and yearly passes.

How to verify your boarding pass

Validating tickets is required prior to boarding. Stamp your ticket at the blue machines at the entrances of subway stations, as well as those on buses and trams, to validate it.

Tickets purchased from the tram or bus driver directly are automatically validated and do not require a second stamp.

Where can I use my ticket?

A portion of Lower Austria, the Burgenland, and all of Vienna are included in the transportation association for eastern Austria. One complete zone, or core zone, belongs to Vienna.

A single ticket is good for one-way travel within a single zone. You may switch to alternative course lines, but you may not halt your progress.

All modes of public transportation, including buses, trams, trains, the BadnerBahn, and the majority of regional bus routes, accept tickets that have been validated.

Using the Subway in Vienna to Get Around

Trains operate approximately every five minutes from five in the morning to midnight, Monday through Thursday and Sunday, and continuously on Friday and Saturday.

Most attractions are accessible by U-Bahn, particularly in the city's core and more populated districts.

At stations, tickets can be purchased from machines or windows. Just keep in mind to insert your ticket into one of the blue machines to validate it before boarding.

If utilizing a day or multi-day pass, you just need to do this once.

From 4:30 am to 1:10 am, the S-10 Bahn's lines operate from railway stations, serving satellite towns and suburbs.

City Walking In Vienna

Arrive ready for plenty of walking on cobblestoned side streets because a large portion of Vienna's inner center is pedestrian-only.

Experiencing Vienna is best on foot, as you can avoid the crowds and get a feel for the atmosphere of each district.

As things stretch out beyond the inner city, you might think about taking public transportation in between walks.

The Best Way
To Travel Around Vienna

Using public transportation and walking are the two greatest methods to get around Vienna. The little InnereStadt is home to a number of historic attractions that are simple to access with just a good pair of walking shoes.

But if you want to visit some of the more outlying areas, the city's bus, streetcar, and subway services will take you there. Taxis are also widely available.

The City Airport Train is one of the many modes of public transit that connect Vienna to the Vienna International Airport.

By foot

The best way to experience this city is by strolling about. In reality, in the Inner City, many of Vienna's historic sites, such as St. Stephen's Cathedral and Hofburg Palace, are only a few steps apart.

Public Transit System

The Wiener Linien, Vienna's convenient and user-friendly public transportation, is excellent for venturing outside of the city. Routes for buses and streetcars wind around the entire city.

Using the same ticket, which is available at every stop, you can switch between modes. A one-, three-, or eight-day unlimited pass costs 2.20 euros, or you can purchase individual rides (prices range from around 7 to 40 euros, depending on the length of validity).

You can use your Vienna Card on public transportation as well. If you manage to miss the final streetcar or bus, you can board one of the numerous night buses (identified with the letter "N") that run along defined routes.

Subway Station

The Wiener Linien also runs the U-Bahn subway system, which serves the city, and the Schnellbahn or S-Bahn light-rail system, which serves the suburbs.

Taxi

In Vienna, taxis are widely available, but you should only use them if absolutely necessary because the costs quickly add up. Before getting inside the cab, agree on a fare; otherwise, you risk being overcharged.

Asking your concierge about transportation costs to and from various locations is another smart move. Uber and other ride-sharing services have a presence in Vienna.

Bike

With more than 150 miles of designated bicycle pathways, Vienna is fairly bike-friendly, similar to many other European towns.

In fact, many Vienna residents choose bicycles over automobiles. Bicycles can be transported for no charge on public transit as well. Rates start at about 40 euros per day, and there are many rental companies in the Prater area and along the Danube Canal.

Car

If you decide to drive yourself, you'll quickly learn why many Vienna residents don't drive: the city's streets are congested and difficult to maneuver, and traffic in the middle of the city can be a nightmare.

Additionally, you won't be able to park anywhere in the central areas without purchasing a parking ticket, which you may do so at the majority of newsstands and cigarette stores.

Waiting to rent a car until you're ready to depart Vienna may help you avoid parking in the city if you're planning a lovely country trip.

There are rental companies at the airport, but they will cost you an additional 6 percent on top of the already high 21 percent tax on all rentals. In the city, prices are lower. A passport and a driver's license that is at least one year old are required in order to rent an automobile.

CHAPTER 4

The Best Places To Stay In Vienna

Vienna is a beautiful city that has been named the best place to live (on earth) for more than ten years straight. This means that you have a wide range of options when looking for the top neighborhoods in Vienna to stay in.

Vienna is not only a fantastic place to live but also the center of culture for the most cultured region in Europe.

This large city is brimming with special vibrancy, charm, and flare. It has amazing infrastructure and is pleasantly safe and clean. More inspiration is available in the city today than you can ever absorb in just one short visit. Indeed, it would take weeks to adequately process it all.

Vienna, which has two million citizens, is located on the famous banks of the Danube River. For everyone who enjoys history, art, architecture, or has a romantic bent, Vienna reveals to be a city of dreams.

It has an incredible variety of viewing options, including attractive medieval alleys, imperial squares, the Imperial Palace, Schönbrunn Palace, the Ring boulevard, and an environment with all of the infrastructure, amenities, and modern conveniences expected of a world-class metropolis.

Vienna is primarily a city with unrivaled culture. This includes everything from traditional theater to experimental, dance and film festivals, to opera and operetta of the highest caliber, concerts, and exhibitions.

Vienna is renowned for its coffee shops, traditional wine taverns, delectable culinary specialties, and cuisine. It is also known as the city of coffee houses.

The following are the top places to stay in Vienna:

1. InnereStadt in district 1

District 1 accolade belongs to InnereStadt, and for good cause. Up until a little over 150 years ago, the whole city limits of Vienna were located in the center.

The neighborhood, which is encircled by the famous Ringstrasse, is protected as a UNESCO World Heritage Site.

Even while it might take you less than an hour to walk from one corner to the next, the sights, sounds, cafes, pubs, restaurants, and cobblestone streets might easily keep you occupied for weeks.

This is the best place to stay in Vienna for visitors who have never been there before in order to view all of the major tourist attractions and places the amazing city has to offer.

The Innere Stadt, the heart of Austria's capital, is still Vienna's original Old Town.

With more than 100,000 employees, this region in Vienna boasts Vienna's highest employment rate thanks to the large influx of tourists.

This area of the city is also home to a number of company headquarters, which helps to increase employment.

There are so many top-notch attractions in this neighborhood. The hotels in this area will be the most expensive and upscale because it is the ideal area for tourists to stay.

Other options to the traditional hotel include apartments and rooms for rent, albeit these will still be more expensive than lodging in any other area of the city.

Where To Stay In The Inner City

- Austria Hotels

- Park Hyatt Vienna

2. Leopoldstadt, located in district 2

The Danube Canal divides the First District from the Second District, which is Leopoldstadt. It is reasonably simple to remain in the Leopoldstadt and frequently visit the First District because they are connected by a few pedestrian-friendly bridges.

With 1,500 acres, the Prater Public Park is Vienna's largest green space. Although it has several tourist attractions and a theme park, the Prater Public Park is ideal for those who want big, open spaces.

Additionally, there are lots of lovely stores and eateries located here.

The Leopoldstadt extends from Vienna's old center to the Danube River up in the northeast.

The most popular attractions in the area, including the Wiener Riesenrad Ferris Wheel, the sand beach along the Danube Canal, and a ton of amazing restaurants, are located in inner Leopoldstadt.

The region also includes the gentrified, formerly run-down Jewish neighborhood. It now acts as a magnet, drawing in younger individuals.

The growth of eateries and hipper coffee shops like the Kleines Café has aided in this.

The region has become a favorite hangout for the middle class as a result, making it one of the more desirable areas of the city to live in and stay in when visiting Vienna.

As the cost of living continues to rise, artists have been driven away.

Where to stay in Leopoldstadt

- Hotel Stefanie

- House of Time

3. Landstrasse in district 3

District 3 is known as Landstrasse. It is located on the Danube Canal's right bank. The enormous Belvedere Palace and Gardens and the Wien Mitte train station are both located on the Landstrasse.

Landstrasse, which borders the Wieden District, is a fantastic location for shopping or leisurely wandering.

The Landstrasse's few significant tourist destinations are located to the neighborhood's north. Here, the Third District meets the First District and the Old Town of Vienna.

The Belvedere Palace and Gardens are still, without a doubt, the Third District's most popular tourist destination. This area of the district, which is unexpectedly fairly affordable, is also the most expensive.

With 80,000 residents, the district's southern regions are well-liked residential neighborhoods.

Except for the St. Marxer Friedhof cemetery, a romantically designed Germanic Regency cemetery, this area of the town is boring to tourists.

Hotel Goldene Spinne Is A Good Place To Stay In Landstrasse.

4. Wieden in the Fourth district

A fairly small neighborhood called District 4 is located south of the city's core. This is a charming area that attracts tourists and is well-liked by artists and students as a place to reside.

The area, which has barely 30,000 residents, also has some ugly post-war reconstructions in addition to a baroque Palais.

Visitors should concentrate their efforts on the streets near Karlsplatz. The iconic Karlskirche Church, which dominates its square as the main attraction of the Wieden District, is among the many noteworthy sights that are concentrated here.

The Karlskirche Church was without a doubt the area's most beautiful structure, yet it was located for a very long time outside the original city walls.

It has recently undergone renovations and is once more adored for the frescoes that adorn it. Even now, the church, which is devoted to St. Karl-Borromao, continues to draw sizable crowds.

The Wien Museum is located nearby on the Karlsplatz.

The capital's municipal museum provides so much more than just this. Visitors may naturally follow the city's history from the Stone Age to the present, but it also has a noteworthy art collection.

Naschmarkt is located just across the corner from this museum and cathedral.

There are a variety of unusual and locally manufactured things available here in addition to fresh meals of all kinds, offering a welcome respite from the region's constant architectural highlights.

In addition to this, the area has a wide variety of entertainment options, including outstanding restaurants, whiskey bars, top-notch fashion boutiques, and flower shops.

Where to Stay in Wieden

- Hotel Kaiserhof and Pakat Suites

5. Margaraten in district 5

Margareten is an infectious and enjoyable Bohemian mood, it offers something distinct from the Old Town's culture and architecture. It is located in the city's center.

Naturally, the district's neighborhoods also feature opulent furnishings and creative flare in addition to the traditional Viennese architecture.

The neighborhood's Naschmarkt outdoor fresh food market also serves foodies of all stripes looking to purchase regionally produced goods at notably favorable pricing.

With the help of neighborhood rehabilitation initiatives, Margareten has been able to establish a reputation as an accessible and reasonably priced neighborhood in the center of Vienna.

It has 50,000 inhabitants and is still expanding and thriving.

The area, which also has character-filled cafes, smaller bars, and independent businesses in the lovely corners of Margareten, is popular with students and young people.

A great place to stay in Vienna is Margareten.

Where to stay in Margareten

- Art Hotel Vienna

6. Mariahilf in district 6

The Mariahilf is another name for District 6. This makes it one of the older districts in today's Vienna, dating back to the 1800s.

The community is located next to Mariahilfastrasse, a popular tourist destination. There are many conventional stores lining the street.

However, Mariahilf itself proved to be a breath of fresh air, very different from the more popular areas.

Instead, it is occupied by small art galleries, cafes, and thrift shops. The enormous Nazi flak tower, an infamous landmark, is located here.

Today, it houses an intriguing private zoo and aquarium.

The existence of the academy contributes to the artistic atmosphere in Mariahilf's eastern section. Because of this, there are innumerable art galleries and businesses that compete for space with specialty shops that sell designer furniture. Lamps and lampshades are traded by unique people.

However, the Flak tower that the Nazis built to protect the city from Second World War air raids dominates the entire region.

The Mariahilfer Church is a stunning baroque pilgrimage church that is worth a visitor's attention.

As it is no longer so near to the Ringstrasse and Vienna's Old Town, hotel rates are lower in this area.

Where to Stay in Mariahilf

-Hotel Beethoven and Leonardo

7. Neubau in district 7

The Neubau is the so-called emerging Seventh District. It has established a reputation for itself in Vienna's nightlife and low-cost lodging.

The Spittelberg and the Schleifmuhglasse compete with one another for the title of coolest neighborhood in the city.

There is a strong and pervasive sense of the university in this area, as evidenced by the numerous street sellers, dive pubs, cafes, and inexpensive restaurants.

The walk to Vienna's downtown takes about 20 minutes, which is a drawback to the cheap lodging options available here.

However, if you're a traveler who enjoys the nightlife and party scene, you can find it by just leaving your hotel and walking down the street.

The Museumsquartier is located here in Neubau near the Spittelberg neighborhood. Visitors can also visit the Zoom Children's Museum, which is excellent for families with young children, on one of the few streets in Vienna where museums follow one another.

On a nice day, you should definitely take a stroll in this neighborhood.

Undoubtedly, the Seventh District is more appealing and dynamic than the inner districts, but at the risk of being a little rough around the edges.

Where To Stay in Neubau

- Pharmador Pension and the Sans Souci Hotel

8. Josefstadt in 8th district

A small neighborhood called Josefstadt, sometimes known as District 8, is located close to the Vienna University, City Hall, and the Parliament building.

The Josefstadt is the smallest neighborhood in terms of population with only 23,000 people, but it is close enough to the major university building and directly behind City Hall to be a fascinating neighborhood occupied by both students and employees.

Unfortunately, it does not serve as a strong attraction for tourists to the area.

Even though the area dates back to the 1700s and the heyday of Vienna and the Austrian Empire, it is mostly residential in nature. The Josefstadt, however, is not without appeal.

Numerous tiny galleries, independent stores, bars, and cafes may be found here. The majority of the student housing is located in the posh eastern section.

The unfashionable red light area next to Gurtel road is home to a sizeable foreigner population on the opposite side, to the west.

Where to stay in Josefstadt

- The Hotel Josefshof and the Hotel Graf Stadion

9. Alsergrund in district 9

The General Hospital is located in District 9, often known as the Alsergrund.

The presence of other academic buildings nearby indicates that the neighborhood's population is mostly either medical professionals or students.

The majority of the region is suburban residential areas, with the exception of the Main Hospital of Vienna and the general university buildings.

The Ringstrasse and murky Gurtel Road encircle it on opposite sides.

The park, which is free to everyone, is enjoyed by members of the public and tourists. A significant portion of the storied private art collection of the Prince of Liechtenstein is on display in the museum located in the main basement structure of the castle.

This magnificent collection, which is nearly unique in the city, focuses on art from the Baroque era.

The combination of the genuine royal structure and the art collection it houses makes for a pleasant tourist attraction, especially given that the castle was just recently renovated.

Where to stay in Alsergrund

- Hotel Regina and The Harmonie

10. Favoriten in district 10

District 10 Favoriten is the most populous district. Austria is actively constructing its new international central train station here.

It is challenging to beat the Favoriten as a cheap place to live or stay in Vienna.

Although it has a high rate of crime without any tourist attractions for a safe city like Vienna, many foreigners live here (because of the inexpensive rents).

Although Favoriten is still very bearable in terms of safety by worldwide standards, the best part of the district is in the south.

The parish churches of Oberlaa and Laarberg are among the many churches in the city that might be worth any additional time that is wasted.

Additionally, a historic water tower from the 1800s is still present. However, the district's southernmost sections tend to be more commercial, residential, and recreational due to the presence of office buildings, apartment complexes, and parks.

Where to stay in Favoriten

- Hotel Schani

11. Ottakring in district 16

In Vienna's northern region is Ottakring. This emerging, multiracial neighborhood has a lot to offer both visitors and locals.

The Gurtel confines it with its constant stream of vehicles. The area seems bustling and interesting from here.

The city's students and young at heart will never run out of places to go—there are plenty of excellent restaurants and bars with fair prices.

The region has recently gained notoriety for its burgeoning Turkish population, which is represented by Turkish and Cypriot restaurants, coffee shops, marketplaces, and bakeries.

Oase is a great restaurant option that offers your daily fill of delicious falafel and fresh baklava.

Where to stay in Ottakring

- The Hotel Hadrigan and The Colony Apartments.

How To Avoid Tourist Traps In Vienna

The Schönbrunn Palace and St. Stephen's Cathedral are just two of the stunning sites in Austria's capital city. However, it is simple to err while moving around Vienna.

1. Not looking into discount card options

You will come across references to cards and passes that you can purchase that will save you money while you research your trip to Vienna.

The Vienna PASS and the Vienna Card are the two most popular ones. For €59, €87, €109, or €136, the Vienna Pass grants you free admission to several attractions for 1, 2, 3, or 6 days, while the Vienna Card entitles you to savings on admission to attractions and concerts as well as in stores, eateries, and cafes.

Nice, huh? It depends, really. If you are really watching your money, you probably spend more than you make.

For some travelers, these discount cards are worthwhile. Take the sightseeing bus and visit a lot of art galleries and museums to save money if you wish to visit several tourist places.

For instance, the Vienna PASS is worthwhile for the majority of travelers if they visit three or more fee-based tourist attractions per day.

If you use the Vienna Card frequently enough, you can also save money, albeit not all of the reductions are substantial.

If you don't plan ahead, you can find yourself spending more merely to take advantage of your discount.

Think carefully about how you want to spend your time in Vienna before purchasing one of these cards. Keep in mind that most activities in Vienna are free.

Interested in visiting the city's art and museums? The good news is that if you're under 19, you can enter most of them without paying.

2. Moving About

Don't take the City Airport Train by following the obvious signage when you arrive at the Vienna airport; instead, proceed to platforms 1 or 2. Travelers on a tight budget can save money by taking the regular train.

The City Airport Train is the quickest method to go to Wien Mitte, however, it only cuts 9 minutes off of the travel time.

Because the other trains stop at more stations, they can transport you to a station that is closer to where you are staying, saving you time.

Keep in mind that you must purchase a ticket before boarding the train.

The city airport train from the airport to WienMitte costs 12 euros and travels in about 16 minutes, whereas the ordinary train costs 4 euros and travels in about 25 minutes, saving you 8 euros even though the trip takes longer.

3. Remaining In Malls

Shopaholics will find a variety of upscale malls and concept stores in Vienna, but it's also worthwhile to visit the vibrant markets.

Riesenflohmarkt for instance in Wienerberg happens every Sunday on the outskirts of the city. When you have to sift through mounds of clothing and home goods, it can seem a little intimidating at first, but with a little haggling, you can find a genuine deal.

In contrast, Nashmarkt is a well-liked flea market in the middle. Along with delicious delicacies like oils, spices, and handmade chocolates, you may purchase jewelry and purses.

4. Sticking to Schnitzel and Sachertorte Only

When visiting Vienna, resist the urge to solely consume the city's well-known cuisine. While in the city, you should also enjoy a variety of other Austrian treats.

Don't forget to try the street cuisine, and follow it up with a glass of regional wine, which is best savored at a wine bar.

Vienna's Top Attractions for Tourists

Vienna Vacation Guide 2023

Vienna is one of the most beautiful towns in Europe, with innumerable museums, castles, and sumptuous parks attesting to its richness and splendor.

Vienna, the nation's capital and cultural hub, used to be the home of the Hapsburg family, whose Emperors and Empresses were avid supporters of the humanities.

As a result, there are many wonderful art collections to discover.

Given that Vienna is associated with renowned composers like Beethoven, Strauss, and Schoenberg, attending a performance at the Vienna State Opera is a must whenever in the city.

An excellent and convenient way to view many of Venice's most popular tourist destinations all at once is to stroll along the Ringstrasse, soaking in all the amazing architecture along the way, before entering the city's actual center.

Visitors will not be short of things to see and do in this city, which stands for sophistication and culture:

1. State Hall

The magnificent State Hall of the Austrian National Library, which was constructed in the eighteenth century, must be seen to be believed; an exquisite statue of Emperor Charles VI, who ordered it, is located in the center.

Numerous old volumes and tomes fill the shelves, and a charming dome with spectacular murals sits above.

The exquisitely carved wooden railings, columns, and banisters complete the space's elegant appearance.

The State Hall is a true feast for the eyes and well worth visiting when in Vienna. You can practically feel the abundance of knowledge pouring from the bookcases.

2. Naschmarkt

The Naschmarkt, Vienna's busiest market, is enjoyable to explore. Its numerous stalls, stands, and shops offer a wide variety of goods, including spices, vegetables, seafood, meats, and clothing.

It is a nice afternoon activity to browse the bustling market. Kaiserschmarrn and Palatschinken are two dishes that are served at many of the area's cafés and restaurants and are particularly well-liked by both tourists and residents.

 The Naschmarkt is a fantastic spot to buy both souvenirs and fresh fruits and vegetables.

3. The Capitol Building

The opulent Parliament Building, which is on the Ringstrasse, was constructed in the Greek Revival design.

The sessions of the Austrian Parliament are held here. Due to democracy's connection to Ancient Greece, classic Greek architecture was chosen; its brilliantly white columns and magnificent bronze statues are beautiful to behold, and the exquisite Pallas Athene Fountain lies in the building's foreground.

The Parliament Building, one of the most well-liked tourist destinations in Vienna, is highly recommended due to its magnificent design and significance to the nation.

4. Saint Peter's Cathedral

The earliest churches on the property date to the Early Middle Ages and St. Peter's Church is located on Petersplatz.

The current church, which was built in the Baroque style in 1733, was inspired by St. Peter's Basilica in the Vatican.

Although the interior is attractive, its beautiful interior, which features wonderful frescoes, is without a doubt the centerpiece. The artwork on the altar, organ, and pulpit is equally lovely.

The church is especially wonderful to visit because it is largely hidden away behind the other structures and emerges majestically before you as though out of thin air.

5. Stadtpark

The Vienna River runs through the expansive Stadtpark, which borders the Ringstrasse. If you've done all the sightseeing you can handle in one day, head to the park for some relaxation.

Visitors will find such well-known individuals as the composer Strauss and the painter Schindler within the display of greenery thanks to the various sculptures and monuments of the great Viennese that are dispersed throughout.

A children's park, concert hall, and groomed gardens, in addition to the abundance of fauna and plants, make it well worth visiting.

6. Stephansplatz

One of Vienna's most significant squares is Stephansplatz, which is situated in the center of the city.

The huge St. Stephen's Cathedral, which rises to an astonishing 136 meters, stands in the heart of the plaza and commands attention.

Stephansplatz is a stunning example of how ancient and contemporary architectural forms can coexist.

The majority of visitors to the city come through at some point because there are so many things to see and do, as well as a ton of stores, restaurants, and pubs that are available nearby.

7. Museum of Natural History

The Natural History Museum in Vienna, which has more than 30 million items, is one of the most significant institutions of its kind in the world.

Everything from dinosaurs and valuable stones to prehistoric art and adorable creatures are included in the 39 exhibition halls.

Its intriguing exhibitions and displays will teach visitors a lot. The magnificent palace itself, which has opulent halls, stairs, and lobbies, is equally spectacular as the extensive collection.

The Natural History Museum, which was constructed in the late nineteenth century and is situated on the Ringstrasse, is identical to the Kunsthistorisches Museum, which is situated right in front of it.

8. Prater

Leopoldstadt is home to the sizable public park known as Prater. It is a well-liked location for both locals and tourists because of its huge green spaces.

An amusement park, museum, and even a disco are located within the park, which many people go to relax and unwind amidst the foliage.

Take a trip on the enormous Ferris Wheel that soars over Prater while exploring the park; the vistas are stunning.

9. The Hofburg Palace

This old palace, which can be found in the heart of Vienna, served as the Hasburgs' primary residence and is still one of the most opulent structures of its kind.

You could easily get lost here for a few days because it resembles a huge, decorated cake. If you only have time to visit one Vienna attraction, make it this one.

10. Central Memorial Park

The Central Cemetery is only a short tram ride from the city's core and resembles a well-kept park rather than a cemetery.

It is well worth visiting for a respectful stroll because it is the final resting place of many famous Viennese people.

11. Amalienbad

The 10th district has an unbelievably magnificent indoor pool. The 1920s-era Amalienbad's architecture was influenced by Roman baths, and its interior artfully combines Art Nouveau and Deco styles.

You can treat yourself to a leisurely swim and a full spa experience for a few euros. Watch the schedule for the late-night pool parties, which include top-notch DJs and light shows.

12. Demel

Since 1786, Demel, one of Vienna's original salons, has been serving confectionery marvels. If you have a sweet tooth, you'll need to be pulled away from this place because there are lavish ring cakes, cream slices, the richest hot chocolate, and an abundance of strudels.

13. Wiener Riesenrad

The enormous Ferris wheel in Vienna is clearly visible from kilometers away. As a gloriously garish fin-de-siècle icon that stands 200 feet above the Prater park, it was constructed in 1897 to commemorate Emperor Franz Joseph's 50 years in power.

As romantic as it gets, watching the sunset over the rooftops and into the Danube from one of the cottages if you're on a minibreak with someone special.

14. Supersense

The city's most fashionable one-stop shop for design. Supersense bills itself as the "home of analog delicacies" and is housed in an art nouveau townhouse.

Here, you can expect to find anything from a functional letterpress to hand-cut vinyl, a perfume lab, and a recording studio.

You can learn about wet-plate ambrotypes while printing some postcards or using a gorgeous typewriter because it's somewhere between a museum and a design boutique.

Even a café that serves delectable cakes and coffee is nearby for subsequent exploration.

15. The Jewish Museum

In 1895, Vienna welcomed the opening of the first museum in the world devoted to Jewish history, culture, and religious activities.

After being closed and pillaged by the Nazis, it was extensively renovated in 2011, then reopened on Dorotheergasse in its present configuration.

16. Albertina

The Albertina, which is situated in Vienna's Innere Stadt, is home to an incredible collection of sculptures, paintings, and drawings.

The Albertina, which has stood since the 17th century and was once a part of the city's medieval walls, was restored into a palace before becoming an art museum. The collection is fascinating to look at and is home to one of the largest and most significant print rooms on Earth.

On display are masterpieces by Toulouse-Lautrec, Bruegel the Elder, and Leonardo da Vinci.

Temporary exhibitions ensure that this is a location worth returning to for both locals and tourists in addition to its lovely permanent collection.

17. Vienna State Opera

Without attending an opera, a trip to Vienna would be incomplete. The Vienna State Opera is the ideal location to go see a performance because the city is synonymous with the magnificent art form.

The opera house, which had been built in 1869 on the Ringstrasse, was heavily damaged by a bomb during World War II, but it was rebuilt in 1955 as the opulent high Renaissance structure that stands before us today.

The theatre itself, as well as the marble staircases, lavish lobbies, and other interior features, are spectacular.

The Vienna State Opera offers daily performances of numerous operas, ballets, and classical concerts, so there is something for everyone to enjoy.

18. Wiener Rathaus

Although there are no wieners served at the Wiener Rathaus, there is a well-known restaurant serving Vietnamese cuisine there.

Instead, it serves as both the town hall and the administrative center for the State of Vienna in Vienna.

The Rathausmann, a statue that stands atop the tower and is a representation of Vienna, is a highlight of the Gothic-style edifice that was built in the 1880s.

A significant refurbishment of the Wiener Rathaus is currently underway and is scheduled to be finished in 2023.

19. Graben

One of the most well-known streets in the heart of Vienna is Graben. The Austrian capital's ancient Roman encampment is where the name "graben," which translates to "trench" in German, first appeared. Back then, Vienna was enclosed by a city wall and had a trench running beside it.

Later, the ditch was filled in and turned into one of Vienna's first residential streets. The Graben was initially an area where craftsmen resided in wooden homes, but over time it changed into a market and then homes for the city's aristocracy.

With many regional delicacies, including Wien Porzellan, it is now an upscale shopping promenade.

20. Ringstrasse

The Ringstrasse is a road that encircles Vienna's inner city and is just over 5 kilometers (3 miles) long.

Many of Vienna's most significant structures, including palaces, museums, and stately mansions, line both sides of the Boulevard and were commissioned in the middle of the 19th century.

The Ringstrasse was built beginning in 1857, and it was inaugurated in 1865.

21. Belvedere Complex

The Belvedere, which includes a number of palaces and an orangery from the late 17th century, is an essential component of Vienna's historic landscape.

The complex was created by Prince Eugene of Savoy for this vacation residence. The palaces housed the French monarchy that was escaping the country during the French Revolution.

The Belvedere offers fantastic views of Vienna and is magnificent to gaze at night when it is fully lit up.

Bobby B. Turner

CHAPTER 4

The Best Activities To Do In Vienna

Vienna is a true cultural hub that has produced some of the world's finest thinkers and artists.

Although it boasts numerous magnificent palaces, cathedrals, theaters, and museums, the city also has a vibrant nightlife, with many clubs and restaurants.

Vienna is the apex of musical heritage. The city was home to several famous musicians, including

Mozart, Beethoven, and both Johann Strauss brothers.

The numerous orchestras, musicians, and vocalists in the city continue to perform their music today.

Ancient villages, classic Austrian towns, and breathtaking mountain landscapes may all be found close to the city.

It would be difficult to visit Vienna and not be in awe of how magnificent everything is.

Here are a few enjoyable activities in Vienna:

1. Wander through the Schönbrunn Palace and Gardens

One of the nicest things to do in Vienna and the first stop for any traveler must be Schönbrunn Palace.

The palace was named after a spring that Emperor Matthias discovered there in 1612. The current enormous Baroque-style palace was once a small hunting lodge, which grew over time.

One of Austria's top tourist destinations is Schönbrunn Palace.

2. Take A Ride On The Wiener Riesenrad

The Wiener Riesenrad is a historic, enormous Ferris wheel that dominates the skyline of Vienna.

If you enjoy rides, arcades, ghost trains, and games, this place has plenty of entertaining activities to keep you entertained for the afternoon.

3. Consider a Food Tour

Are you interested in Austrian cuisine? The national dish of Austria, schnitzel, is well-known to most people, but they are generally unaware of its other culinary offerings.

A terrific approach to discovering the most well-known foods in Vienna is to take a culinary tour.

Hire a local guide to tour you around the city as you venture there. Visit the best neighborhood restaurants to sample traditional appetizers, entrées, and desserts.

4. Take in the sights at Vienna's old town

There are bustling cafes, restaurants, museums, and art galleries in this area.

Visit famous sites like the Hofburg palace and St. Stephen's Cathedral, or go shopping on the pedestrianized KrtnerStrasse.

5. Visit Kaiserliche

There are royal and religious treasures there, as well as crowns, jewels, clothes, and one of the biggest emeralds in the entire world.

An extremely old narwhal tooth that was mistaken for a unicorn horn and designated a Habsburg heirloom can be found among the items.

6. Go to Tiergarten

This zoo was founded in 1752. 8,500 creatures from more than 700 species live there.

From a raised gallery, guests can observe giraffes, as well as orangutans, Koalas, Siberian tigers, and African elephants.

Yang Yang and Yuan Yuan, a couple of giant pandas, are the zoo's most popular residents. The building of the zoo has a distinctively vintage aspect that enhances the ambience of the location.

7. Visit the Natural History Museum to view dinosaur skeletons

One of the top museums of natural history in the world is Vienna. Its amazing artifact collection, which includes ancient meteorites and dinosaur skeletons, is housed in an equally spectacular structure.

8. Segway City Tour: Explore the Area

Take a segway tour for a fun and original way to explore the city. No prior knowledge is essential; segways are a simple mode of transportation for everyone.

9. Take a bike trip to discover the city like a resident

10. Visit Kahlenberg Mountain to go hiking

One of the most well-liked day trip locations from Vienna is Kahlenberg Mountain. It is close to the city by bus or automobile and is situated in the heavily forested Vienna Woods.

The Stefaniewarte tower at the summit offers a fantastic view of the entire city as well as areas of Lower Austria, making it a lovely place to go trekking.

11. Kayak on the Alte Donau for the day

12. At Wiener WiazHaus, try the wiener schnitzel

In the city, Wiener WiazHaus debuted in 1898. Vienna is well known for serving excellent schnitzel and beer. The eatery has a modest, simple retro aesthetic.

There are two outside garden spaces, a parlor and taproom inside, and the old wood bar is still there.

Veal wiener schnitzel is the most popular dish at Wiener WiazHaus, but there are three menus to select from, each with vegetarian options.

Romantic Things To Do For Couples In Vienna

With good reason, Vienna is regarded as one of the most romantic cities in the world. Beautiful city squares and gardens, well-preserved palaces, and museums make up the city's magnificent display of Austrian opulence.

The classical music of Mozart, Beethoven, and Brahms regularly serenade your romantic strolls across the city.

Enjoy a private tour of fairytale Habsburg palaces and coffee shops lighted by chandeliers. Waltz down the azure Danube or experience regal fancies in palaces straight out of a fairytale.

Here are some fantastic date suggestions for couples in Vienna that take into consideration the city's most romantic spots to help you discover your sense of romance there.

1. Go to the Belvedere and look at The Kiss

Inside a baroque mansion, find lovely artworks. Prince Eugene of Savoy's vacation residence is the baroque Belvedere Palace, which dates to the 18th century.

It houses an impressive collection of artwork, including symbolist pieces by Austrian painter Gustav Klimt.

The intriguing The Kiss, also known as The Lovers, by the late painters is hidden away in the Upper Belvedere's galleries.

The mosaic-like painting shows a couple kissing passionately in a flowery field as they stand on the edge of a cliff.

The clothing of the lovers is covered in gold leaf. Flakes of gold, silver, and even platinum cover the background as well.

There are private excursions available that will teach you more about the history and the paintings.

2. Take a boat trip on the Danube

The greatest place to view the Danube river is on Vienna's long, narrow island known as Donauinsel (Danube Island).

One of Strauss's well-known waltzes was inspired by the Danube's grandeur, and the river's winding through Vienna is in fact beautiful.

A fantastic place to learn about the river is the small, grassy island to the east of the center. There are walking pathways that follow the riverside, as well as beaches where paddle boats designed for two people can be rented.

3. Travel across Vienna in a carriage

Aside from the air being filled with well-known classical songs, Vienna is also known for its distant hoofbeats on cobblestone streets.

From your hotel in Vienna, you may arrange a memorable tour of the city on a classic horse-drawn filker carriage.

When InnereStadt's landmarks and lovely walkways are bathed in golden light at night, a spin is at its most romantic.

4. Learn to waltz together

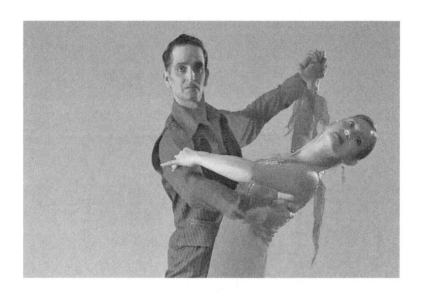

A date out in Vienna can be more memorable by picking up some moves through a waltz class together.

During the three-month season, which typically begins in November and peaks between January and February, the waltz's birthplace hosts hundreds of balls. Joining one might be the ultimate Viennese experience.

No matter the ball season, there are numerous classes in the city where you may learn to waltz. It includes the Tanzschule Elmayer. It offers 50-minute classes for couples.

5. Split a chocolate spa service

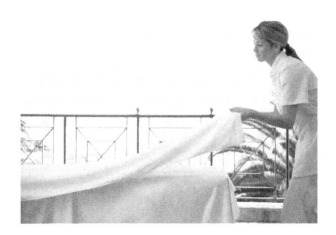

The café of Hotel Sacher Wien is located in the same building as the Sacher Boutique Spa, where you can truly indulge in chocolate.

A rich chocolate wrap, a detoxifying cacao peeling, a chocolate body mask, and a soothing massage utilizing body care products containing chocolate are all included in their 90-minute Symphony in Chocolate treatment.

6.   Watch a ballet at Vienna State Opera

Vienna State Opera House dates to the 1860s, and it's still as magnificent as it was over a century ago.

It has a lavishly frescoed and decorated grand entry hall, as well as elegant intermission rooms. The best seats average between €100 to €200.

7.   Book a candlelit dinner at Le Ciel

Restaurant Le Ciel by Toni Mörwald is an award-winning restaurant in Vienna. Besides holding a Michelin star, the restaurant also achieved 3 toques and a near-perfect score of 18 from Gault Millau.

You do need to book ahead to enjoy this fine dining moment by candlelight.

The prices tend to be on the higher side for Vienna, but it's one of the go-to spots to impress. Choose lunch at its outside terrace for a more casual ambiance.

Street Food In Vienna

Whether you are visiting Vienna to taste some delicious authentic Austrian dishes, or to admire Vienna's art galleries, museums, architecture, and classical music, you can't go home without trying some of the best street food in Vienna.

Streed food in Vienna is quite popular. The Viennese are bringing their specialties to the streets and making this great food affordable for everyone who appreciates street food.

It is one of those European cities where you find food stalls on every corner, especially during the holiday season.

Don't be surprised if you can't find fast food like pizza, as the streets of Vienna are filled with sausage stands.

The Best Street Food Vendors in Vienna

1.   Bitzinger

Just within a 2-minute walk from the Vienna State Opera, you can find the best Viennese sausage in town. Viennese sausages are part of the Austrian culture and are a favorite street food to locals and tourists alike.

There is nothing like a late-night sausage with bread and mustard from one of the most famous street food places in town.

In Bitzinger, you can find all types of sausages. Bitzinger is located at Augustinerstrasse 1, Vienna 1010, Austria.

2.   Blue Mustard

Located just in front of the Blue Mustard restaurant in the city center, is one of the best food trucks in the city.

While the restaurant and the cocktail bar inside are something worth checking out if you have the time and money, this cheaper and faster substitute is excellent and will satisfy all your needs.

The Airstream food truck offers modern street food and starting from up to $12 you can get anything from salads, soups, homemade lemonade, burgers, and many more.

Wash down this delicious food with a cold beer, and you are all set for the day.

Located at Dorotheergasse 6/8, 1010 Wien, Austria.

3. Wurstelstand

Visiting Vienna you can't help but eat sausage, sausage, and more sausage! If you are looking to experience street food as the locals do, then join the long line in the very first sausage stand in Vienna, founded in 1928.

Food starts at less than $4, and you can choose anything from their 60 dishes.

Try the cheese-filled Krainer sausage, as it is always in demand. If you are vegetarian but your friends insist on eating here, don't despair.

Wurstelstand offers a large variety of vegetarian food, starting from a veggie burger, onion rings, french fries, sweet potato fries, veggie bombs, and others.

Thirsty customers can refresh with a large selection of beers, soft drinks, wine and spirits.The sausage stand is open till the wee hours of the morning, perfect for a quick bite after clubbing.

Located at DöblingerGürtel 2, 1190 Wien, Austria, and open Mon-Sat from 10 am to 04 am, and Sun 12 pm to 2 am.

4.   Yong Streetfood

Hop on the train to find this great eatery! Located within a short walking distance from Naschmarkt near the city center, is Yong Streetfood.

It is one of the best in Vienna, where you can find the tastiest Asian street food. Their menu offers a mix of Korean, Chinese, Taiwanese, and Japanese dishes.

Asian food lovers are welcome to try any of the variety of dishes from Jianbing to beef kimchi tacos to vegetarian dishes, you are well covered.

But you won't be able to find fried noodles or miso soup here. If you want cheap, quick, and delicious street food this is the place, just right off of the crowded Naschmarkt.

The owners are Mandarin-speaking but speak little English, and there is limited sitting.

Located at 1040, RechteWienzeile 9A, 1040 Wien, Austria.

5.   Oriental Sandwich Bar

Oriental Sandwich Bar is located in the busy city center surrounded by many other eateries. If you are looking for oriental, high-end street food, this is the perfect place.

The founder comes from the south of Egypt and brings with her traditional recipes that have been passed from generation to generation and combine them with European tastes.

The results? Mouthwatering wraps and sandwiches prepared on-site, such as fresh falafel wraps made with light, tasty and crisp falafels, crushed lamb beef balls, Oriental pasta, Mediterranean wraps, and more great food, vegetarian and vegan included.

If you are in the city center, you have to stop by and enjoy the atmosphere in this lovely place or grab your food to go in a nice takeaway box.

Located at Rotenturmstrasse 27, Vienna 1010 Austria.

6. Maroni Street Stands

Roasted chestnuts are yet another Vienna street snack that you simply must sample while there.

A common winter pleasure offered at the so-called Maroni stalls is this snack. Roasted chestnuts are referred to as Maroni in English.

They can be found all across Vienna, but they tend to cluster around the city's top tourist destinations.

If you are visiting during the Christmas season, be sure to pick up some roasted chestnuts because they are a cheap snack.

Another common street snack in Vienna is roast potato wedges, which you may encounter while strolling the streets and touring the city. similar to a slice of pizza in the US.

7. Hungry Man

Hungry Guy serves international street cuisine and is situated on a side street in Schwedenplatz, also known as Sweden Square.

The combination of their Eastern Mediterranean cuisine and Western flavors draws both locals and tourists from throughout the world.

In order to create some of the best international street food in Vienna, The Hungry Guy team brings together some of the top street food cooks from Iraq, Italy, Jordan, Israel, Germany, and Austria.

If you're strolling around the city center, stop by the most well-liked location and take in a pleasant atmosphere. Order a Viennese schnitzel on Arabic bread for meat lovers, or falafel on freshly baked pita bread with hummus for vegetarians.

Your appetite will be satisfied by anything on the menu, and some items are even less than $10.

Located at Rabensteig 1, 1010 Wien, Austria.

8. Gorilla Kitchen

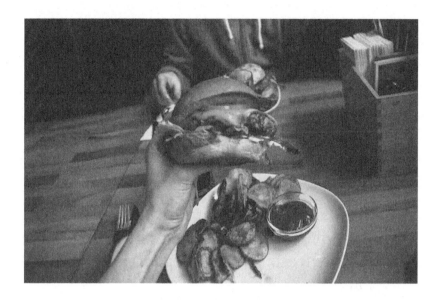

Stop by Gorilla Kitchen if you're looking for a change of pace from Viennan food and want to pique your taste buds with some chile and heat.

There is a huge variety of Mexican food available, including burritos, tacos, burrito bowls, your choice of salsa, guacamole, nachos, quesadillas, and everything else you can think of.

Avegadillo, a tofu lotus, or a mangold chickpeas burrito bowl are all delicious vegetarian options.

Located at Gußhausstraße 19, 1040 Wien, Austria.

Where to Go for the Best Street Food in Vienna

1. Naschmarkt Street Food Market in Vienna

Locals will direct you to Naschmarkt if you inquire about the best street food in Vienna. Naschmarkt, which dates to the 16th century, is not only Vienna's oldest market, but also its largest, with more than 120 food stands.

There are many different types of international meals available, including Turkish, Arabic, Asian street food, fresh fruit and vegetables, tea, olives, beef, and much more.

That's not all, either! There are several bars and restaurants all around this lively and constantly packed Camden Market in Vienna. Naschmarkt, which is close to the city's heart, is the ideal place to go for some late-night street cuisine with your pals.

When in Vienna, you must visit one of the top places for street cuisine.

2. Schwedenplatz

The Schwedenplatz, often known as Sweden Square, lies in the heart of Vienna. From Subway on one end to McDonald's on the other, there are street food vendors on every corner.

There are also places to get doner kebab, Asian food, pizza, sausage, and, in the summer, the best ice cream in town. This is the perfect place to go for simple, delectable food after a day of shopping.

CHAPTER 6

The Biggest Festivals In Vienna

Planning a trip to Austria? While you're in Vienna, don't forget to check out a couple music and film festivals.

Here is a selection of a few well-known Vienna festivals that might provide you with a wonderful experience and give you a glimpse into Vienna's rich cultural diversity.

1. Resonanzen Festival

Music has become much more popular today than it was in the past when it was played on instruments that were historically accurate. The Resonanzen Festival is one of Vienna's most cherished music festivals because of this.

Vienna celebrates Renaissance, Baroque, and Medieval music for nine days each January.

The Resonanzen Festival is a must-attend event for everyone who wants to experience the ancient sounds of recorders, harpsichords, guitars and lutes in Europe.

Leading orchestras from around the world congregate under one roof each year to perform on various topics.

2. Viennale

The Viennale international film festival, which has been held annually in October since 1960, is the premier international cinema occasion in Austria.

The various historic movie theaters in Vienna, including the planetarium Urania Sternwarte, Gartenbaukino, Filmmuseum, Stadtkino, and Metro-Kino, show a wide variety of movies.

The Vienna International Film Festival presents a selection of recently released films from Austria and other nations.

This program premieres the best experimental cinema, short films, and documentaries from around the world, from Buenos Aires to Cannes.

The Viennale Film Festival also includes special occasions, gatherings, gala screenings, audience debates, interviews, and opportunities for attendees to mingle with festival visitors from across the world.

3. Donauinselfest

This is one of the best events in Vienna, and is generally in full swing throughout its three-day summer run.

The Donauinselfest festival, which takes place on Danube Island, provides a weekend of entertainment, music, and mornings with foggy eyesight.

You can sing and dance to a variety of pop stars and radio stations. This event features music from a variety of genres, including rap, rock, pop, electronic music, hip-hop, metal, and folk.

In addition, there are a variety of different activities to keep you busy each day, as well as several kiosks selling mouthwatering food.

4. Voice Mania

The Voice Mania, one of Vienna, Austria's most thrilling and vibrant festivals, strikes the city when the November fog rolls in.

You get to hear incredible singers from Europe and elsewhere. The "Bel Canto" singers open the performance with gospel songs, yodlers, arias, and electrifying sounds and rhythms from the many balconies in Vienna's city center.

However, the Theater in Spittelberg only hosts a small number of concerts.

The Best Bars in Vienna

In practically every sense, the Austrian capital is grand, and its steadfast dedication to a fun night out is equally striking.

The top bars in Vienna range widely, from seedy dives to cutting-edge cocktail lounges, not to mention glittering rooftops and more. No matter the hour, a decent drink is what Vienna is all about.

The greatest pubs in Vienna are ready to help you unwind, whether you're exhausted from exploring the city's numerous attractions and prestigious museums or you've simply sampled enough coffee and cake to last a lifetime.

1. Miranda Bar

This location is a grammarian's paradise, a symphony of pastel pink, marble, and ornate pineapples. However, Miranda possesses both elegance and substance; come this way for a night of creatively crafted cocktails.

These are some very stylish and inventive cocktails, but they are also reasonably priced.

2. Loos American Bar

This mirrored, wood-paneled bar from 1908 makes you feel like you're entering a jewelry box.

The staff will reward you with some of Vienna's best traditional cocktails if you show them that you're serious about sticking for a drink despite the fact that it's a tourist hotspot.

3. Kleinod

A cocktail bar with a roof terrace decorated in the style of the 1930s becomes the place to be seen in the summer.

Look no further for a sophisticated, glitzy evening. Kleinod evokes the heyday of the cocktail with its Art Deco design, a ton of dark wood, and chandeliers, but the mixology here is startlingly modern.

One thing to keep in mind is that, like in many Austrian pubs, smoking is permitted inside.

4. Top Kino

An arthouse movie theater with one of Vienna's most welcoming and relaxed bars. Make a night of it by ordering tickets to a movie.

It's excellent value, as you would anticipate from a place that draws a youthful, alternative clientele. The toasties make wonderful blotting paper, and the craft beer selection is very impressive.

5. Blaue Bar

This location is quite exquisite. The crew here knows everything there is to know about creating top-notch cocktails.

If you limit yourself to one and avoid extravagant champagne cocktails, you can have a fantastic time.

6. Das Loft Bar & Lounge

This elegant establishment, located on the 18th level of the Sofitel Vienna Stephansdom, offers stunning views of the city as well as a menu of polished takes on traditional dishes.

It's hard to beat watching the sunset over the rooftops while holding a glass of something powerful and cold.

Try the Plata Roja with tequila that has been infused with saffron or the special gin concoction with cherry tomato, lime, and basil syrup.

You have to dress up and pay for a setting like this, but it's worth it.

7. Onyx Bar

Onyx, is a stylish design hotel on the sixth level, with floor-to-ceiling windows that will give you the impression that you are standing on the top of St.

Stephen's Cathedral. The choice of spirits produces almost as many gasps as the vistas.

With sparkling wine as its base, you'll be able to sample your way through one of the most extensive cocktail menus in the city.

The Best Parks To Visit In Vienna

Austria offers the perfect climate for a gorgeous, juicy green environment because of its location in the center of Europe.

The parks in Vienna are great for day trips or just taking a break from the city. The nicest and most intriguing green spaces in the Austrian capital are highlighted in this guide.

1. City Park

The Vienna City Park, the city's first public park, was constructed between 1860 and 1862 and debuted in August of that same year.

Josef Selleny and Rudolf Siebeck created it, and it is built in the design of an English landscape garden.

The park was formerly on the left bank of the River Wien because it was merely a portion of the city's first district.

However, the park was expanded and a new section was constructed on the other side of the river a year later.

Today, this park in Vienna has the greatest number of monuments and sculptures. Johann Strauss' memorial is unquestionably the one that has been most frequently photographed.

2. Danube Park

This park served as a pistol shooting range for around 70 years before going abandoned. This land was refurbished and turned into a neighborhood recreation area in the 1960s.

It was unveiled in 1964 at the Vienna International Gardening Show alongside its architectural icon, the 252-meter-high Danube Tower.

Nowadays, there are many skateparks, playgrounds, and public tennis courts.

It is the ideal location for viewing sculptures by well-known international artists, participating in sports, and unwinding in the meadow.

3. Lainzer Tiergarten

This region has been inhabited since Roman times, and it was turned into a hunting area throughout Austria's imperial era.

The Vienna Woods' Lainzer Tiergarten is currently a public nature preserve. There is a significant amount of wildlife in this park, including deer, roe deer, and wild boars. In addition, it is a well-liked destination for day trippers, families, and hikers.

Additionally, the Hermesvilla, a center for culture and exhibitions, is open to everyone with an interest in culture.

4. Volksgarten

In Vienna's first district, on the Ringstrasse, is a public park called the Volksgarten. The park was constructed between 1819 and 1823, and it consists of two distinct architectural styles.

The Hofburg's side was built in the English style, with a sparse tree population. On the Ringstrasse side, however, the park was built in the French baroque style, with a meticulously planned garden.

This park has sculptures, just like every park does. Visitors can locate there, for instance, the memorials for Franz Grillparzer and Empress

Elisabeth, as well as the Theseustemple, which is a scaled-down reproduction of the Temple of Hephaistos in Athens.

Rose enthusiasts will also find their preferred flower there.

5. Burggarten

The Burggarten is a park that is a great starting place for exploring some of Vienna's most significant sights.

Visitors can discover the Palmenhaus, which has a restaurant and a butterfly house, in the park itself.

There is a tiny, calm pond there as well as various statues of well-known Austrians.

6. Prater

The Prater's woodlands and meadows spread between the Danube canal and the Danube, a favorite of generations of Vienna residents.

Previously used as hunting grounds for the Habsburg monarchy, this old river basin is now Vienna's most well-liked park for strolling, biking, and summertime picnicking.

Along the Hauptallee boulevard, which leads to the Lusthaus, a 16th-century hunting lodge that was converted for imperial festivities in the late 18th century and now houses a café and restaurant serving Austrian classics in opulent chandelier-lit splendor, stately chestnut trees stand watch.

7. Schloss Belvedere

Schloss Belvedere offers even more splendor in the form of imperial gardens. Between the two

Belvedere buildings are grand three-tiered baroque gardens decorated with neatly trimmed topiary and planned out in symmetrical formal French design.

8. Wienerwald

The Wienerwald (Vienna Woods) covers more than 1000 sq km of Vienna's western border (386 sq miles).

Vineyards, picturesque Heurigen (rustic wine taverns), and an abundance of mountain biking and hiking routes wind through the woods and up into the hills.

CHAPTER 7

Vienna's Must-Try Dishes and Where to Find Them

There are numerous delectable regional specialties to be found in Vienna.

Locavores will particularly value the emphasis on top-notch produce and fresh, locally produced products used in many local restaurants and cafés.

These are the finest dishes to taste in Vienna, from sausages and substantial soups to delectable cakes and schnitzel:

1. Würstel

There are Würstel stands virtually everywhere in Austria. They are unavoidable! It's so good that I still have dreams about the Wurstel I had in Vienna. It certainly is Vienna's best Austrian cuisine.

Pork and beef are combined to make Wurstel, a sausage. Typically, a sheep's gut surrounds it. Before being served, Wurstel is smoked!

There are several locations to purchase Wurstel, but Bitzinger is the one I personally suggest, and there's an excellent reason for it. Since nothing costs more than €4, it is incredibly inexpensive.

2. Apfelstrudel

Apple strudel, or apfelstrudel, is exactly what it sounds like. This is a fantastic dessert that we enjoy in the US, but since it's Austrian in origin, it tastes even better there.

Apple strudel has a superior apple pie flavor. It is an apple pie with a thin pastry crust encasing apples, brown sugar, and cinnamon. To finish it off, sugar is typically sprinkled on top.

The dish may occasionally be accompanied by whipped cream or ice cream.

There are several locations in Vienna where you may sample apple strudel, but I personally suggest going to the Hofburg Cafe. Conveniently, this cafe is a part of Hofburg Palace.

3. Wiener Schnitzel

Schnitzel is a regularly served dish in restaurants and cafes throughout the city that is really popular and simple yet delicious, and even kids usually enjoy it.

You may try wiener schnitzel in a variety of locations throughout the city. Try any eatery in the area!

4. Sachertorte

The Austrian capital's proud emblem is the Sachertorte.

I suggest buying sachertorte at the Hofburg Café, which is a component of Hofburg Palace, just like the apple strudel.

5. Austrian Goulash

This hearty beef stew you'll probably have in Vienna frequently has dumplings and is seasoned with tomatoes, onion, and paprika.

A dish like this is ideal on a chilly winter day.

This meal is offered at Café Mozart and Puerstner, both of which are renowned for their delectable preparations of it.

6. Knoedel

Knoedel, a common meal in several Central European nations, is essentially cooked dumplings.

As a side dish to other traditional dishes like the Saint Martin Goose in November, they are typically made of flour or potatoes.

Although meatballs in a soup can also be served with Knoedels in Austria, the real skill of Viennese handicraft is in converting them into desserts.

These can be found on the menu of practically every coffee shop in Vienna and are usually filled with soft cheese, jam, apricots, or plums.

This lunch is available at the Landtmann Cafe on Ringstrasse.

7. Tafelspitz

Tafelspitz, an authentically Austrian meal created with soft filets of beef or veal gently simmered in broth, is another regional specialty for meat aficionados.

This meal is popular across the nation, especially in the fall and winter.

It is highly recommended that you sample it at PlachuttaWollzeile, a renowned eatery noted for serving this well-known meal close to St. Stephens Cathedral.

The Best Restaurants In Vienna

Vienna's top eateries are a delectable celebration of the city, and the city's gourmet sector is even beginning to challenge those renowned cafes for first place.

There is no shortage of gastronomic marvels in this area, from award-winning Japanese restaurants to historic pubs serving traditional Austrian cuisine.

These portions can be somewhat substantial, so be sure to bring an appetite.

1. Lugeck

The family that owns and operates the renowned Schnitzel restaurant Figlmüller also runs Lugeck, which is housed in the beautiful Regensburger Hof structure.

Austrian classics and a variety of international meals are available at this gastropub interpretation of an old-school wine bar.

2. Motto Restaurant and Bar

Don't be shocked if you spy a few visiting A-listers among the chic regulars because it's a terrific place for people-watching.

Motto looks the part with its stark walls and luxurious green velvet seats, and the aesthetics are complemented by first-rate cuisine. Try their sophisticated spins on classic dishes like strawberry nougat dumplings and Tafelspitz.

3. Erich

An underground bar/restaurant in the incredibly hip 7th area. You might easily stroll right past Erich, which is nestled away on the side of Sankt-Ulrichsplatz.

This restaurant checks all the boxes around the clock when it comes to dishes.

4. Mochi

The most well-known Japanese fusion restaurant in Vienna specializes in mouthwatering sushi and sashimi.

It takes some work to get a table here, but it's worth it because every bite is delicious. The staff is also outstanding.

5. Pizza Randale

Randale, formerly a gritty tavern, has been brought to life with its decor and inventive pizzas.

It is virtually impossible to be unhappy here. The atmosphere is relaxed, and the food is great.

6. Palmenhaus

The renowned botanical hothouse in Vienna, which has a view of the elegant Burggarten grounds, is also a brasserie open all day.

This restaurant combines Austrian and Mediterranean cuisine. Positive memories are certain.

7. Ulrich

From first orders to the last, Erich's sibling restaurant is bustling and lively and consistently provides great pan-European dishes.

Although it's frequently crowded on the weekends, it's also excellent for weekday dinners.

This is the spot to be for brunch.

CHAPTER 8

Money Saving Tips For Vienna

1. Purchase breakfast from the supermarket

Vienna doesn't really do breakfast or brunch. Finding cafes or restaurants where you can actually get breakfast can be difficult and expensive.

Despite this, you get a fantastic chance to save money. Vienna is filled with bakeries and grocery stores, so grab a croissant and some fruit to eat on the road. Both time and money will be saved!

2. Travel to Vienna off-season

If you want to travel on a budget, you should be too. I am a HUGE fan of wintertime European city breaks.

Winters in Vienna can be quite chilly, and it lacks the ambiance of Austria's ski resorts. Because of this, the most cost-effective season to visit Vienna is during the winter.

That's because Vienna experiences its lowest tourist season from January through February.

You can explore Vienna without the annoying crowds, and prices are much lower as well. There are more options and hotels are much less expensive than in the summer.

3. Have Käsekrainers for lunch

A large hotdog called a Käsekrainer has bits of melted cheese inside the sausage. The sausage vendors that offer them can be found all over the city; it's the best kind of street cuisine to come out of Vienna.

These are not only very excellent but also very reasonably priced. They will fill you up and typically cost around €4.50.

Additionally, they are convenient for eating on the go, giving you more time to explore.

4. From the airport, take the regional train

The City Airport Train is a complete rip-off! A one-way ticket costs €12, and a roundtrip ticket costs €21. It is definitely intended to snare inexperienced tourists.

A single ticket for the basic train is priced at €4.

5. Do not use the travel pass

Walking through Vienna's city center is one of the finest ways to get to know the place and experience the ambiance because it is simple to navigate on foot.

There are 24- or 48-hour transport cards available for purchase in Vienna, but unless your accommodation is incredibly far away, they are just not necessary.

Though buying a transport pass could seem like a good way to save money, chances are you won't use it frequently enough to make it worthwhile!

On that topic, remember to purchase your tickets at the machines in the stations rather than on the tram or bus in order to save money when using public transportation.

On board, they always cost more.

Don't get taken off guard, too! Always remember to validate your machine-generated tickets by stamping them at the blue machines located at the entrances to subway stations, as well as on buses and trams.

Bobby B. Turner

CHAPTER 9

The Ideal Itinerary For A Week In Vienna

This is a city that has transformed to a fashionable artistic paradise.

Numerous museums, palaces, markets, restaurants, odd art displays, and delectable cuisine halls can be found in Vienna.

It is also a short rail ride from Bratislava.

Here is how I would arrange a week-long visit to Vienna, given all it has to offer:

Day 1

Make Use Of A Free Walking Tour

This is a wonderful opportunity to experience the city's atmosphere, get a glimpse of its history and culture, and learn how to navigate on foot.

Additionally, you are free to ask your guide any and all questions.

Visit the Fine Arts Museum

The majority of the objects come from the old Hapsburg collection. There is at least enough to keep you occupied for a few hours at this more "classic art" focused museum.

Visit the Spectacular Vienna State Opera

Opera is essentially always associated with Vienna as it is a fundamental part of life in Vienna With over 1,700 seats, it was finished in 1869. You may take a behind-the-scenes tour of the structure and discover its significance and history for just 9 EUR.

I suggest purchasing last-minute standing-room tickets for a show for about 10 EUR (often less) on the day of the performance, often 60 to 80 minutes before the start of the performance.

Day 2

Explore The Museumsquartier

A number of festivals are held at the Museumsquartier throughout the year. Basically, you must visit this place if you enjoy modern art!

Enjoy Schonbrunn Palace

There are free gardens here and a lovely maze. This is a wonderful place to take children.

Make a trip to the natural history museum

The museum has one of the largest collections in all of Europe with approximately 30 million items.

There is a digital planetarium in the museum where you may view films on the earth's history. Visitation is strongly advised – it's both entertaining and educational!

Day 3

Visit The House of Music

Exhibits here were founded in 2000 and feature world music displays as well as replicas of some of the earliest instruments ever made by humans.

There are even virtual stages where you can conduct your own symphony and original texts and artifacts that you can view.

Check out Jewish Square

Vienna had a substantial Jewish population for centuries. The Nazis then arrived.

Travel to The Albertina

Given that there are many museums in the city, The Albertina is one of the better ones.

It is located in one of the Imperial Palace's former wings for individual residences. It is most well-known for its print collection, which includes 60,000 drawings and more than a million prints.

Day 4

Visit the Belvedere Palace

The Belvedere, which was constructed in the first half of the eighteenth century, is actually made up of two palaces. Incredible art is housed in the northern palace.

A changing exhibition space is called the southern palace. The free grounds are ideal for a stroll on a fine day because they have lovely fountains, gravel pathways, ponds, statues, plants, and flowers.

Check out The Freud Museum

From 1891 through 1938, Sigmund Freud, the well-known creator of psychoanalysis, resided in this flat, which is now a museum.

There are now movies from his private life in this museum. It is compact and may be explored in one hour or less.

Promenade along the Danube

Stroll alongside the Danube. With a length of approximately 2,900 km, it is the second-longest river in Europe.

There are a few little "beaches" where you may unwind during the summer and enjoy the sunshine.

Day 5

Visit the Mozart stadium

To commemorate Mozart's death's 150th anniversary, the museum was inaugurated in 1941. Numerous artworks, artifacts, letters, and other items from his life are also displayed here. Check out this cute small museum.

Check out the Imperial Palace

This enormous structure, which features numerous attractions, was constructed in the 13th century.

You could easily stay here for half a day. The Imperial Residences are the first; they actually combine three attractions into one: the Sisi exhibit, which celebrates the revered Empress Elisabeth of Austria's life, the silver collection, which includes hundreds of pieces of royal china, and the actual royal apartments.

The Imperial Treasury is my favorite area. Numerous crowns, scepters, and other royal items are displayed here, along with a very thorough history of the Hapsburg dynasty and empire.

You should absolutely purchase the audio tour even if it is not free. It gives the exhibits a ton of additional background. Really, all you need to do is view this attraction to have learned enough!

Explore Naschmarkt

This is the biggest outdoor food market in Vienna. It has been in operation for hundreds of years (since the 16th century) and has a wide selection of eateries, street vendors, and supermarkets.

It has a great ambiance and, on a warm sunny day, it's nice to relax outside with a meal and a bottle of wine.

However, it is a touch touristic (don't go food shopping here). There are still a lot of residents here despite its fame. Visit Umarfisch for some wine and seafood.

Day 6

Do a wine tour

Take a bike trip in the nearby Wachau Valley you'll have the opportunity to sample some of the greatest local wine. It's a full-day excursion that includes some sightseeing and lunch (allow 8–10 hours for it).

Day 7

Visit Bratislava

From Vienna, a day trip to Bratislava is highly recommended. Since Bratislava's city is quite compact, getting around on foot is simple.

Regular trains leave Vienna for as cheap as 10 EUR, while bus fares start at about 4 EUR.

THANK YOU VERY MUCH FOR READING

HOPE YOU FOUND THIS BOOK HELPFUL, IF YOU DO, KINDLY LEAVE A POSITIVE REVIEW OR RATE IT ON AMAZON.

Other Books By The Author

- Mexico Travel Guide 2023 - Discover Top Attractions, What and Where To Eat, Where To Stay, The Best Things To Do, The Perfect Mexican Itinerary & Why You'll Love Mexico

- Bahamas Travel Guide 2023 - The Essential Step-By-Step Guide To The Bahamas, Discover Top Attractions, The Best Things To Do, Where To Stay & Learn How To Live Like The Locals

Printed in Great Britain
by Amazon

24780606R00109